Make Waves

Make Waves: A Kid's Devotional on Changing the World
Published by Parent Cue, a division of The reThink Group, Inc.
5870 Charlotte Lane, Suite 300
Cumming, GA 30040 U.S.A.

Interested in buying devotionals for the kids in your church or community? Get discounted rates on quantities of 10 or more at parentcuestore.org or orangestore.org.

ISBN: 978-1-63570-181-4

©2022 Parent Cue

Author: Kellen Moore

Lead Editor: Lauren Terrell
Creative Direction: Ashley Shugart
Project Manager: Brian Sharp
Director of Parent Cue: Hannah Joiner Crosby
Director of Publishing: Mike Jeffries
Design & Layout: Kingery Design Co.
Illustration: Shane Kingery
Framework: 252 Kids Team

Printed in the United States of America
First Edition 2022

1 2 3 4 5 6 7 8 9 10

03/24/22

A Kid's Devotional on
Changing the World

KELLEN MOORE

COWABUNGA!

What's up?! I'm Kellen, and I get to be your number one cheerleader while you read this devotional.

First, what *is* a devotional? Simple! A devotional is a book that helps you get closer to God! There it is, short and sweet.

If you've never read a devotional before, welcome! We're going to have so much life-changing fun over the next few weeks. If you're an expert devotional reader, you may think you already know what's in store . . .

→ A fresh, new topic each week

→ Four devotional days plus a bonus challenge each week

→ Fun activities for you and all your favorite people

→ The answers to all life's biggest questions

. . . and you're not wrong! Well, maybe a little too hopeful with that last point. I can't promise to answer *all* your burning questions, but you *will* learn how to be more like Jesus and create BIG change in the world around you over the next nine weeks.

If you're like I was as a kid, chances are, you just read *nine* weeks and almost closed the book. But, wait! We aren't learning in a memorizing-the-multiplication-table kind of way. I promise to make it more fun than that. In fact, interaction is the name of the game. The more you follow the tips, the more fun you'll have, and the more you'll get out of this book!

First tip: If you're excited about reading this book, find the nearest friend, family member, or leader and tell them, "I am so pumped about reading this book called *Make Waves!* Also, this writer named Kellen is super cool!" (Aww, thanks!)

Now, let's talk about the title: *Make Waves.* No, this isn't an instructional manual about swimming, even though swimming is awesome.

This book is all about making waves of change around us. God designed each of us to be uniquely capable of creating change by how we treat others at home, school, and in the world. The best part is, when we follow Jesus (who made huge waves everywhere He went), we don't have to do it alone!

When Jesus went to Heaven, He left the Holy Spirit to be with us. He gave a whole big speech about it that you can read in John 14:26. But what does that mean?? Later on, this guy named Paul traveled to different countries teaching people how to be Christ-like or "live in the Spirit." He explains the Holy Spirit this way to the people of Galatia:

> *The fruit the Holy Spirit produces is love, joy and peace. It is being patient, kind and good. It is being faithful and gentle and having control of oneself.*
>
> *Galatians 5:22-23a*

The Holy Spirit is God's Spirit—like actually God! The Holy Spirit! It is all the wonderfulness of God and Jesus living inside each of us. And just like apple trees produce apples, we are like God trees who produce God's fruit! The Holy Spirit produces God's fruit in us, and it comes out as love, joy, peace, patience, kindness, goodness, faithfulness, gentleness, and self-control. All these qualities of God's fruit are choices God wants us to make, even when we don't feel like loving someone or having joy. That's why Jesus sent the Holy Spirit to live inside of us—to help us make those right choices!

As we jump into this book and make a splash, there is one last thing that I must mention . . .

WHISTLE

SWIMMING BUDDIES!

Sorry for yelling, LOL. One thing you should know about me: I grew up in California. Yes, *that* California. The state that takes up most of the west coast and borders the Pacific Ocean. Which means I practically grew up at the beach and the pool. And as every kid in California knows, when you go swimming, you need a swimming buddy!

A swimming buddy is someone who can help you out when you need it or is there to remind you, "You got this! Just keep swimming!"

So, before you dive into this devotional, pick one grown-up swimming buddy you really like and trust. Maybe that's a parent, aunt, uncle, coach, or small group leader. Maybe that's the person who gave you this devotional.

Tell that person you're starting to read this book—that you want to make it all the way through, but you might need their help. (Here's where you get to assign work to a grown-up.) Tell your grown-up swimming buddy that one way they can help you is by memorizing one Bible verse or passage with you each week.

You'll find the Memory Verse at the beginning of each week. (It's called the Memory Verse Challenge.) Check-in on your grown-up swimming buddy's progress throughout the week. Then, at the end of the week, sign off on whether your grown-up completed the challenge (whether they memorized the verse or verses). Feel free to give them prizes when they do! (Might we suggest: doing extra chores, a five-minute back rub, or a piece of candy from that secret stash under your mattress?)

Alright, it's finally time to . . .

JUMP IN AND MAKE WAVES!

WEEK ONE

Love

DAY 1

WHAT IS LOVE?

We're starting our nine-week adventure with a word you hear everywhere and probably say all the time: *LOVE*.

In the verse we read in the introduction, love is listed as the first quality of the fruit of the Spirit. It takes the lead on how we see and treat other people, ourselves, and God. In fact, love is *so* important, some say it's impossible to have the other qualities of the fruit of the Spirit if you don't have love! So, let's talk about love for a minute.

What is your definition of L-O-V-E? See if you can think of four words to describe love and write them in the spaces below:

_____   _____

_____   _____

There's a reason there have been so many songs, movies, and books made about love. From Anna and Hans singing "Love Is an Open Door," to a young lady losing a glass slipper as her prince searches for her in Cinderella, love is sung or talked about everywhere.

That's because love has such a huge ripple effect on the world. Your love for someone else moves that person to love another person, and so on and so on, spreading like the ripples created when you throw a pebble into a lake. And you know what else love does? It makes joy, peace, patience, kindness, goodness, faithfulness, gentleness, and self-control a lot easier.

Stretch that love muscle by listing five people you really love and what you love most about each one:

1. _____

_____

2. _____

_____

3. _____

_____

4. _____

_____

5. _____

_____

WHISTLE

Get your swimming buddy because here comes your very first . . .

MEMORY VERSE CHALLENGE

Love is patient, love is kind. It does not envy, it does not boast, it is not proud. It does not dishonor others, it is not self-seeking, it is not easily angered, it keeps no record of wrongs. Love does not delight in evil but rejoices with the truth. It always protects, always trusts, always hopes, always perseveres. Love never fails.

1 Corinthians 13:4–8 NIV

DAY 2

HOW DOES GOD SHOW LOVE?

Before we begin day two, go drink a nice cup of cold water. Then come back to this book. I'll wait . . .

. . . No seriously, go grab some water and chug (no cheating, soda doesn't count).

Got water? Checklist:
☐ CUP   ☐ WATER   ☐ COLD

Welcome back! How was it? I hope it was delicious! Water is such a wonderful thing. Not only is it fun to splash in, but it's also super important for our health. And psychiatrists (brain doctors) have even linked it to improving our mood!

God knew how important water would be to the earth and us humans. So God created the oceans, lakes, rivers, ponds, and even rain. Water was *so* important, God covered most of the earth's surface in it. **Take a guess on how much of the earth's surface is covered in water. Circle one:**

20%   50%   70%   90%

Well, before I tell you how much, let's talk more about why God gave us so much water.

God designed all living things to need water (Genesis 1:11-13, 20-26). Fish need it as a home; plants, animals, and people need it to live and grow. From the very beginning, God thought about everything we might need and provided it in big ways—now that's love!

Sometime after God created the first humans—Adam and Eve—they sinned. And their sin had a ripple effect. But it had like, a *bad* ripple effect, not like the good love ripple effect we talked about earlier. Because once sin entered this world, humans kept on sinning. That sin hurt God—kind of like a betrayal. If you have ever been hurt by a sibling or friend, you understand a little of what God might have felt.

Even though we had hurt God, God still showed us love. One of the greatest ways God demonstrated that love was by sending *more* water.

The Living Water.

I know what you're thinking: "God made a giant water monster, like from *Spider-Man: Far from Home*?!" . . . Well, not exactly.

In John 4:10, Jesus, the Son of God, described the living water as a gift from God. Jesus was saying our physical need for water is just like our spiritual need for Jesus. Just like water keeps us alive on Earth, Jesus gives us eternal life with God.

God so loved the world that he gave his one and only Son. Anyone who believes in him will not die but will have eternal life.

John 3:16

God sent Jesus to die for our sins so we can be forgiven. And after Jesus went to Heaven, the Holy Spirit was sent to be with us.

God made some serious waves by sending Jesus.

The ripples of God's love continue to affect people two thousand years after Jesus died. We now have access to God-sized love. And we can share these waves of God's love with others!

On a scale of 1–10, how does it feel to know that the God who made everything loves you in such a big way?

WIPEOUT   RADICAL!

1   2   3   4   5   6   7   8   9   10

Take a minute to talk to God. Close your eyes, write a prayer, or go for a walk so you can talk to God out loud. Whatever feels most comfortable. God hears you no matter how you pray. If any questions or feelings come up while you're praying, talk to a grown-up (maybe the one who's working on memorizing those 1 Corinthians verses about love with you).

Also, Earth's surface is made of 70% of water. See, I told you I'd let you know!

DAY 3

HOW CAN LOVE
MAKE WAVES IN MY LIFE?

What's the gnarliest* thing you've ever found on the beach?

*Gnarliest: surfer word for wildest, strangest, grossest, coolest, etc.

If you've never been to a beach, what's the gnarliest thing you've found in a park or your backyard? Draw what you found and title your drawing below:

The ocean can wash up some pretty cool stuff. But it can also wash stuff away. Have you ever come across the remains of what looked like a really cool sandcastle? Sometimes it's so washed away, you can barely tell it was ever there at all. The ocean has completely erased it.

In the Bible, Peter, one of Jesus' besties, wrote:

> *Most of all, love one another deeply. Love erases many sins by forgiving them.*
>
> *1 Peter 4:8*

When I read that second sentence, it makes me think of ocean waves smoothing out the sand on the beach, making it look new and pristine each day.

Of course, Peter is talking about sin, not sandcastles. Sin is another word for the bad decisions we make. Lying to a parent. Mistreating a friend. Any selfish choice that makes us and others feel bad. Peter says that LOVE is so powerful it washes those sins away completely. Like the waves of the ocean washing the beach clean. *Love erases many sins by forgiving them.*

When Jesus was about to get arrested and killed, people asked Peter if he was friends with Jesus, and he denied it. In that moment, Peter sinned. He made a bad decision. Then he kept on making bad decisions by denying he knew Jesus two more times.

But when Jesus came back to life and showed God's love to Peter by forgiving him, it was like a wave crashing to shore, erasing all the sandcastles—or bad decisions—Peter had made.

The awesome thing is, you can do the same. Love can help you forgive others, and when you love others (including yourself and God), it's like having endless waves clearing the beach! And here's the deal: People will always make mistakes (yes, including you), but because of the gift of the Holy Spirit, we have help making waves of love that erase sin.

Find a piece of paper and a washable marker. Write down a few bad decisions people you love have made (choices they made that hurt you). Think about those people and your love for them. Put the piece of paper in a bowl of water for about ten minutes and let the water wash those bad decisions away.

Of course, forgiveness isn't always that easy. But like the verse from 1 Peter says, your love for others is powerful enough to erase many sins. After ten minutes, look at that soaking wet piece of paper and think about what it would feel like to start fresh with the people you love. **How might you use your love for these people to erase the hurt they caused you?**

MAKE WAVES

DAY 4

HOW DID PEOPLE IN THE BIBLE SHOW LOVE?

What would you rather receive: $200 today or $0.50 a day for two years? Circle one:

A. $200 today

B. $0.50 a day for two years

Well, if you circled A, congrats! You just earned yourself $200! But if you chose B, you just earned yourself enough for a decent surfboard: $365! A little change goes a long way. It may take some time to see that change, but when you do—when you think about where you started and where you are now—it's not so little.

Jesus knew all about how a little change can make huge waves. In the book of Luke, Jesus told a story about a man who made waves by showing love to a person who was different from himself.

Jesus' story begins with a man who was traveling from Jerusalem to Jericho when he was attacked by a robber. This robber took all his clothes, beat him up, and left him there to die. This thief made some bad decisions. But traveling down that same road was a priest (a religious man). When the priest saw the hurt traveler, he kept walking—another bad decision! Next, a Levite (he was also a religious man) walked by and saw the man. If you think he stopped to help . . . nope. He passed by on the other side of the road. *Another* bad decision!

This is where the story gets interesting. A Samaritan man walked down the road next and saw the man on the ground. Now, Jesus was telling this story to a group of people who didn't think highly of Samaritans. Some even hated them, but Jesus continued the story.

The Samaritan stopped to take care of the traveler's injuries by cleaning and bandaging them. The Samaritan then put the man on a donkey and took him to an inn, or hotel, to continue taking care of him. Before the Samaritan left, he paid the owner of the inn to keep taking care of the man.

Talk about making waves of change through showing love to someone! This Samaritan sounds like he understood the power of God's love for others.

Why do you think Jesus chose to share this story with this group of people?

    A. The people needed a bedtime story.

    B. Jesus wanted to make all the priests feel bad.

    C. The people needed to understand how to love others who are different from them.

    D. The people needed to write a book report.

Why is it important to show love to the people everyone avoids?

    A. Every person needs to be loved.

    B. Every person is important to God.

    C. Love has the power to change someone's whole life.

    D. All of the above.

How would your life be different if you showed love to everyone just because they are *someone*?

    A. You would have a lot more friends.

    B. A couple of friends might start treating you differently.

    C. You would spend less time trying to figure out who to like and who to avoid.

    D. You would worry less about who liked you and why.

    E. All of the above (and more).

Jesus told this story because He wants us to learn from the example of the Samaritan and know that love has the power to make waves of change in people's lives.

DAY 5

MAKE WAVES

Wow! We started this week off talking about how the word *love* is one of the most famous words of all time and there's good reason for it. We hear the word *love* used in so many different ways about so many different things or people. "I love cheese pizza!" "I love you, Mom!" "I love you, Babe; will you marry me?" Love is used so many different ways and means a couple of different things.

How are pizza love, Mom love, and kissy love different?

_____

_____

_____

_____

Love is such a popular word because it's more than just a trendy expression; it's a feeling. It's a pretty strong feeling you sometimes can't help but act on. Just like when you're sad, you want to cry, or when you're full of joy, you want to laugh and dance! Because love is such a strong feeling, it'll make you want to get up and do something!

We're designed to love others, to love ourselves, and to love God. Think of some ways you can show someone they're loved? What are ways you can love yourself? And what are some ways to love God?

Ways to love others:

1. _____

2. _____

3. _____

Ways to love yourself:

1. _____

2. _____

3. _____

Ways to love God:

1. _____

2. _____

3. _____

MAKE WAVES CHALLENGE

Congratulations! You did one of the coolest things by completing your first awesome week of this devotional! (Pat yourself on the back and say, "Great job!")

WHISTLE

Time to grade your Swimming Buddy!

DID YOUR GROWN-UP DEVOTIONAL BUDDY MEMORIZE 1 CORINTHIANS 13:4-8?

☐ YES   ☐ NO

✗ ....
(sign your name here)

BONUS:
What did you give them for memorizing the verses?

WEEK
TWO

DAY 1

WHAT IS JOY?

Welcome back! Let me see your beautiful smile! **Take this book in front of a mirror and draw a portrait of your smiling face—because this week, we're talking about joy!**

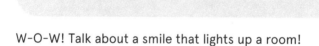

W-O-W! Talk about a smile that lights up a room!

Joy is more than just smiles, laughter, and happiness when everything is going your way. It's easy to be happy when things are good, but real joy comes in good times and bad. Real joy means choosing joy no matter what's going on.

There are a lot of things in this world that can make us feel sad, worried, or even angry, but Jesus sent us His Holy Spirit to help us choose joy even in those hard times.

The Holy Spirit can help you find joy when you were expecting 15 friends at your birthday party, but only three friends showed up. Or when you worked hard on a school project and received a failing grade. Or when you were told a fun trip was planned, but it ended up getting canceled.

Write out a time in your life when things weren't going well, and you needed to choose joy, even though it was tough:

_____

_____

_____

Even though there may be times in our lives when it's tough to choose joy, let's remember what Jesus offers us—His joy! In the book of John, Jesus said,

> *I have told you these things so that you will be filled with my joy. Yes, your joy will overflow!*
>
> *John 15:11 NLT*

In those times when you need joy the most, remember Jesus has filled you with His joy—the kind of joy that's always with you because it comes from someone who's always with you: Jesus!

WHISTLE

Okay, your Swimming Buddy really started off strong. They must LOVE you a lot because last week's verses were not easy to memorize. I think they will be JOYFUL—in more ways than one—to see this week's Memory Verse . . .

MEMORY VERSE CHALLENGE

"Always be joyful because you belong to the Lord. I will say it again. Be joyful!"

Philippians 4:4

DAY 2

HOW DOES GOD SHOW JOY?

Taking trips to the beach was always a really fun experience when I was a kid. I always wanted to bring all the stuff I needed to create the perfect day: towels, toys, sunscreen, umbrellas, lunch, a frisbee.

Draw a sun next to all the items you'd take for your perfect beach day:

Towel	Beach chair
Sunscreen	Swim trunks
Skateboard	Sunglasses
Phone	Dog
Surfboard	Siblings (be nice)
Lunch	Football
Flip flops	Water
Frisbee	Bucket
Book	_____
Portable speaker	

The funny thing is, almost every time we set out on this perfect day, something would happen. We wouldn't be able to find parking; it would rain or be super cloudy; we'd forget a toy at home; sand would get in our food (I like crunch in my sandwich, but not with real sand . . . eww.) My family would have a choice to make: find joy in the fact that it's still a beach day or get upset about the imperfect moments scattered throughout our day.

Creating the perfect day is challenging, but imagine creating the perfect world and people for these perfect days. Remember, God created our world, including people like you and me! We are created in God's image, and God saw that we were really good. But then people started to show that, even though we were created in God's image, we weren't perfect. Sometimes we were the sand on that sandwich (sand + sandwich = no thanks), but that didn't surprise God. God knew we would have flaws and make mistakes and—from time to time—sin. But check out what the Bible says about God's joy:

The Lord your God is with you. He is the Mighty Warrior who saves. He will take great delight in you. In his love he will no longer punish you. Instead, he will sing for joy because of you.

Zephaniah 3:17

We will all do things we're not proud of or make choices that aren't the best, but this is where God is the best example of choosing joy no matter what's going on. God loves us.

God loves you. No matter what mistakes you make, God will continue to love you and sing for joy because of you.

When I think of God singing for joy because of us, I think of that moment at the end of the movie *Trolls*. The lead troll, Poppy, starts singing "Can't Stop This Feeling" with her fellow trolls even though she knew their world wasn't prefect. It's really cool to picture God doing the same: singing a joyful song about us, even though we aren't perfect. (And it brings me an extra spark of joy thinking about God with bright pink troll hair. Hey, it's possible! No one knows what God looks like.)

Below, write out a song and draw a dance you imagine God uses and does to delight in you:

Song:

_____

_____

Dance:

DAY 3

HOW CAN JOY MAKE WAVES IN MY LIFE?

In order to become a stronger swimmer, you need to make your body stronger. Some ways you can do that are:

- → Kicking while holding the ledge of the pool
- → Swimming with a buoy between your knees
- → Holding a kickboard while kicking across the pool
- → Using swim fins or paddles to create more resistance as you swim

When you were learning how to swim, what were some things that helped you get stronger? If you haven't learned to swim yet, or you enjoy a different sport more, what are a few ways you've gotten stronger at whatever exercise you enjoy doing?

_____

_____

_____

_____

Just like when you exercise, your body helps you become a stronger swimmer, knowing you have God's joy inside you makes you a stronger person. The Bible tells us,

> Don't be . . . sad, for the joy of the Lord is your strength!
>
> Nehemiah 8:10b NLT

In life, there are things that will make you hurt, sad, angry, or even frustrated, but the Holy Spirit is with you always, to help you through those times and to help you find joy on the other side. Those feelings may hurt for a while, but they won't last forever. And when they feel like they will, remember, the joy of the Lord gives you strength. You can continue to trust in God because God will always make waves in your life.

The cool part about waves is that the ripples they make can keep going if the waves are large enough. And the spirit of joy makes waves so large they can affect those around us too!

Have you ever found something funny when you're around your friends and everyone began to laugh, and then that laughter brought more laughter? After a while, you're just laughing at the other person laughing! That's the effect that waves of joy can have on everyone around you.

When you spread joy, it will catch on. If you ever see a friend or family member who is in need of some joy in a hard time, ask God to put joy in their life and reach out to bring them the joy you have in your heart.

Remember the song that you wrote down yesterday? The one you imagine our joyful God singing? Play it for your friends or family and start a dance party! If the fun wants to continue, keep the dance party going with everyone's favorite joyful songs!

DAY 4

HOW DID PEOPLE IN THE BIBLE SHOW JOY?

The Bible has a lot to say about joy, but my favorite joy story is found in Acts. **Grab your Bible or Bible App and read Acts 5:17–42.**

You done? Let's discuss.

Jesus taught people some really incredible stuff while He was on Earth. Before He went back to Heaven, Jesus told His closest friends to tell the world about His great love. The people who did that are called the apostles.

When the apostles were in Jerusalem, they were arrested by Jewish leaders, *twice*!

These Jewish leaders never really liked Jesus or those continuing to preach about Him. So, they had the apostles arrested and ordered them to stop preaching in Jesus' name. The crazy part was, during their time in jail, the Lord sent an angel to set them free—thanks, God! But the angel told the apostles to go right back to preaching Jesus' message when they got out—wait, you mean the thing that got them arrested in the first place?

The apostles kept trusting that the Lord had called them to tell everyone about Jesus. So, the apostles left the jail cell and continued to share the Gospel (or Good News). The apostles were determined to keep sharing about Jesus and making huge waves in Jerusalem! And that's just what they did!

But while they were out preaching the *second* time, the Jewish leaders noticed they were not in jail and ordered them to be arrested, again! Talk about things not going their way. This time, the apostles faced the courts. After the court talked it over, some of the religious leaders wanted to put the apostles to death, but one Jewish leader decided to flog them (or beat them) and let them go, ordering them not to preach in Jesus' name ever again.

So, was the Lord with them? It may not have seemed like it at first glance. Arrested. Twice. Beaten. Silenced. But . . . verse 41 says they *were full of joy* when they left the court. Full of joy? After all that? Verse 41 goes on to say *why* they were so happy: They were honored to have suffered for Jesus. The Lord was definitely with them. How else could the apostles have chosen to have joy not only in the middle of all that suffering, but *because* of all that suffering?

One of the best ways to find joy is by remembering the things in life that bring us joy. Take a few minutes to write down some things that bring you joy—like the family God has given you or a close friend who you love being around. Once you create your list, write it on a notecard. Put the notecard in your backpack or tape it to a place where you'll see it often. Read this card the next time you need a reminder of the joy in your life!

DAY 5

MAKE WAVES

As we wrap up this week talking about joy, I want to make sure we take a moment and smile. **On the count of three, we're going to smile together! One . . . two . . . three . . . SMILE!**

In case you're wondering, yes, I smiled too. We're in this together! I am so grateful for you! Speaking of gratefulness, did you know that being grateful goes hand in hand with joy? Being grateful has been proven to increase our positive emotions! But that's nothing new. Humans knew this to be true even thousands of years ago:

Always be joyful. Never stop praying. Give thanks no matter what happens.

1 Thessalonians 5:16–18a

So, to wrap up this week, let's make a Joy Jar.

Materials:

- ⇀ 1 (empty and cleaned out) jar*
- ⇀ 1 piece of paper
- ⇀ Marker(s)
- ⇀ Scissors & tape
- ⇀ All the decorations (optional)

* This can be an old peanut butter jar, salsa jar, mason jar, or any empty jar you can find with a lid.

Start by decorating your jar. Use your piece of paper, marker(s), scissors, and tape to cover the original label with one that says "Joy Jar." Decorate your label however you want.

Then, cut strips of paper and write down things you're grateful for. Leave a stack of paper strips next to your jar and challenge your family to write down things they're grateful for and put them in the jar too.

The next time you get in trouble, feel angry, or feel sad, go to your Joy Jar. Pull out a few strips of paper and remember all the things you have to be grateful for, all the reasons you have to find joy.

MAKE WAVES CHALLENGE

Right on!! Week two of your *Make Waves* devotional is complete! (Now is the time to stand up and dance for joy!)

WHISTLE

Time to grade your Swimming Buddy!

DID YOUR GROWN-UP DEVOTIONAL BUDDY MEMORIZE PHILIPPIANS 4:4?

☐ YES   ☐ NO

✕ ....

(sign your name here)

BONUS:

What did you give them for memorizing the verse?

_____

_____

_____

WEEK THREE

Peace

DAY 1

WHAT IS PEACE?

Before we start this new week, I want you to create a list of all the things you might be thinking about while reading this. Anything from schoolwork to chores to your little brother or sister bugging you:

_____   _____

_____   _____

_____   _____

_____   _____

_____   _____

Great! Now that you have all that written out, let's focus on nothing!

"What's that?" you may be asking. "How do you focus on nothing?"

Well, you caught me, we aren't going to focus on COMPLETELY nothing. Instead, we'll focus on our breath and creating a moment of peace. So, go and find a quiet place, a sibling-free zone. **Once you are done, draw a shaka* sign anywhere on this page!**

> *The shaka sign is used in Hawaiian and surfing culture. It expresses "Thank you," "Things are great," "Right on," and "Take it easy." And it's easy to do. Curl your middle three fingers while extending your thumb and pinky finger—it's also the "Y" symbol in sign language.

When you're ready, spend the next couple of minutes sitting in silence. To prepare yourself, get in a comfortable position. Take three deep breaths. Breathe in for a count of six and breathe out for a count of eight. Good! Again, in for six, out for eight. One last time . . . awesome.

Now, imagine a peaceful place. Real or made up. Be as creative and personal as possible. When I think of the word *peace*, I picture a warm evening with a cool breeze coming off the ocean and the sun setting over the Pacific. *That* is the perfect, peaceful, calm environment for me. What's yours? If you love the woods, imagine leaning back against a strong tree. If you love your grandma's house or the swing in your backyard or the top of a mountain, go there in your mind. Focus on the smells, sounds, and sights of your peaceful place.

Set a timer for two minutes, close your eyes, and just chill out in that peaceful place inside your mind.

Now, write down what you felt during those two minutes and how you feel now:

God created you with great detail. One of those great details is your brain. You have the ability to think about so many things all at once. It can be helpful at times but not very peaceful. All the new and different information we're taking in at all times can sometimes feel overwhelming, but the Bible tells us:

Don't worry about anything. No matter what happens, tell God about everything. Ask and pray, and give thanks to him. Then God's peace will watch over your hearts and your minds.

Philippians 4:6-7a

This week, we're going to uncover what it means to have real peace throughout our lives, whether we're sitting on a beach watching the sunset or running late for school. So get ready for God's peace to wash over you and make waves in the world around you.

WHISTLE

Okay, your Swimming Buddy really started off strong. They must LOVE you a lot because last week's verses were not easy to memorize. I think they will be JOYFUL—in more ways than one—to see this week's Memory Verse . . .

MEMORY VERSE CHALLENGE

"Always be joyful because you belong to the Lord. I will say it again. Be joyful!"

Philippians 4:4

DAY 2

HOW DOES GOD SHOW PEACE?

Picture yourself sitting on a surfboard in the ocean or in a small boat on the lake. The sky is that perfect blue, not one cloud as far as the eye can see. The weather is a wonderful 82 degrees and all you hear is peace and quiet, so you just lay out and enjoy the sun.

Now if you're starting to doze off because I am amazing at describing the best nap moments . . .

WHISTLE

. . . WAKE UP!

You're laying out in the sun just enjoying life until you look up and see dark clouds out of nowhere. BOOM! Thunder sounds, and just like that—you're caught in a crazy storm.

What do you do? Circle the option you would choose:

1. Start swimming/paddling as fast as you can.
2. Signal everyone on the shore with an emergency flare (don't ask where you got it from).
3. Panic and yell, "HELP"!
4. Keep chill-laxing; it's all good.

I know what you're thinking—that went from zero to a hundred real quick. And it did! Sometimes life is the same way. One day everything is going your way. It's nice and peaceful, but the next day, that friend isn't your friend anymore. That one decision at school puts you in detention. Your parents are no longer together. The storms of life come out of nowhere.

And life has been like that since, well, the beginning of time. In Mark 4, the Bible tells us about a time the storms of life caught Jesus' disciples by surprise—literally. Jesus and the disciples were chillin' in a boat, crossing the Sea of Galilee, when out of nowhere . . .

> *A wild storm came up. Waves crashed over the boat. It was about to sink. Jesus was in the back, sleeping on a cushion. The disciples woke him up. They said, "Teacher! Don't you care if we drown?"*
>
> *He got up and ordered the wind to stop. He said to the waves, "Quiet! Be still!" Then the wind died down. And it was completely calm.*
>
> *He said to his disciples, "Why are you so afraid? Don't you have any faith at all yet?"*
>
> *They were terrified. They asked each other, "Who is this? Even the wind and the waves obey him!"*
>
> *Mark 4:37–41*

That's wild! The wind was loud, the waves were high, and everyone on board was so frightened. Jesus was in a storm that threatened the lives of all His friends. And Jesus calmed the storm.

But how? How was He able not to let the storm shake Him, when everyone else was so scared?

The key is in the question Jesus asked His friends: *"Don't you have any faith at all yet?"* (Mark 4:40). The disciples were focused on how big and scary the storm was. Jesus wanted them to focus on how big and powerful God is.

Nothing, absolutely nothing, is bigger than God. There are plenty of "storms" in life that are bigger than us, yes. And we get scared when something is bigger than us. That's okay! Because God is bigger than all the storms. God holds the planets in place. God is good. We can rest knowing God is in charge.

What are some storms currently in your life?

Remember our Memory Verse from yesterday? Take a minute now to practice what Scripture tells us to do in the middle of life's storms. Tell God everything. Pray, ask Him for peace, and thank Him for all you have to be thankful for. Sometimes, when I do this, I can literally feel God's peace washing over me like a refreshing wave. See if you can too.

DAY 3

HOW CAN PEACE MAKE WAVES IN MY LIFE?

Tear a corner of this page off or, if you're like me and get stressed just thinking about ripping the pages of a book, find a piece of paper and tear a section off. Then, tear that piece into two medium-sized pieces. Now, get some tape and try to tape those two pieces back together perfectly—like they've been one big piece all along. Once you're done, tape it to this page here:

TAPE HERE

On a scale of 1 to 10, how difficult was it to tape the two pieces together perfectly?

SUPER EASY   **VERY DIFFICULT**

1   2   3   4   5   6   7   8   9   10

Could you do it better if you had more time or better supplies? Or does it make you want to just throw it away?

Fixing something that's broken isn't always the easiest of tasks. That's why we invented duct tape. Because duct tape fixes everything, unless it doesn't . . . in which case, we throw the thing away and buy a new thing. We aren't always the best fixers. Because fixing something can be messy. It's not always pretty.

There are a lot of things to fix in this world. At one point, there was the *whole world* to fix. That's why Jesus came—to fix the whole world. There wasn't enough duct tape in the universe to fix the mess we had gotten ourselves into.

Sin had broken the connection between us and God. Things were looking pretty bleak. But did Jesus throw the world away and buy a new one? Nope.

"In this world you will have trouble. But be encouraged! I have won the battle over the world."

John 16:33b

Fixing this world wasn't easy. It was a hard battle to win. But Jesus made it possible for us to connect with God again by dying for our sins. That's a huge deal.

So, if the battle is won, why doesn't life feel peaceful and happy all the time? Because sin is still there making things feel chaotic and crazy sometimes. But because of Jesus, we can go to God with that crazy chaos. Because of Jesus, we have access to God's peace. Because of Jesus, we have the encouragement and hope of knowing God has already won the ultimate battle.

This week, when you see a friend or family member struggling to find peace, remind them of what Jesus tells us in John 16:33. In this lifetime, we will face hard things. But because of Jesus, we have access to God's peace, the kind of peace that washes over us always, every time we ask.

MAKE WAVES

DAY 4

HOW DID PEOPLE IN THE BIBLE SHOW PEACE?

So far this week, we've talked about why and how you can have peace in any situation by asking God to give you peace—the peace Jesus helped to make. But what about using that God-sized peace to help others have peace? What about *making* peace in the world around you?

In the book of 1 Samuel, the Bible tells us about a woman named Abigail who did just that.

David (yes, the same David as King David. He just wasn't the king, yet) moved into the desert with all his men. For a little while, he and his men helped guard the sheep of a man named Nabal. Nabal was a wealthy man with 1,000 goats and 3,000 sheep (that's money in the bank in those days). One day, David heard that Nabal was shearing his sheep[1]. And that involved a huge party and lots and lots of yummy food.

So, David sent some of his men to give Nabal a greeting of kindness and ask him to take care of David's men just as David had taken care of Nabal's men and sheep in the past. Nabal didn't respond well. He was rude and refused to take care of David's men, saying, *"Why should I give food to men who come from who knows where?" (1 Samuel 25:11).*

1   giving them a haircut

When David heard what Nabal had said, he got very angry and gathered a few hundred men with swords to visit Nabal (as you can imagine, the men with swords were not coming for a friendly visit this time).

This is where Abigail came in! Abigail was Nabal's wife, and when she heard of Nabal's disrespect, she wanted to make it right, to help make peace. So Abigail put together tons of food, and loaded it up on the backs of donkeys to deliver to David and his men.

When Abigail met David's men coming toward Nabal, she asked David to forgive her husband's foolishness. David accepted her offerings and called his men back. He told Abigail, "Go home in peace. I have heard your words. I'll do what you have asked" (1 Samuel 25:35).

That day Abigail was a peacemaker. She made waves by seeing a situation that needed some peace *fast*, and she took action. She found a way to help defuse a potentially very tense conflict. Seriously, these dudes were ready to go to battle over some rude words. It's actually a pretty incredible story, and as your biggest cheerleader in this book, I highly encourage you to take a few minutes to read the whole thing in 1 Samuel 25.

God uses all kinds of people for all kinds of purposes. In the moment we just read about, God used Abigail to make peace. And God created you to change the world by making small waves of peace, just like Abigail.

You can help others make peace in so many different ways. You can show the world around you what it means to apologize and ask for forgiveness when you've messed up and hurt someone. You can show the world around you what it means to forgive someone who has hurt you. You can show the world around you how to choose peace over revenge.

Just like Jesus brings us peace and can calm our storms, we can bring peace to others even when our storms are raging.

Every family and friend group tends to have a peacemaker. Who do you know who seems to be a natural peacemaker? Who are the people you can totally hear saying, "Okay guys, can't we all just chill for a minute?"

What if everyone in your family or group of friends or on your team was committed to keeping the peace? How would that make a difference in your life? How would that make waves in your world?

DAY 5

MAKE WAVES

Breathe in.

Breathe out.

Peace is such an important part of the fruit of the Spirit because sometimes life can feel crazy or too heavy. When we're in those moments, we can ask God to help us have the Spirit's strength to seek peace. God wants us to lean on the community we have around us when we feel overwhelmed.

Remember your swimming buddy? The one who is memorizing Scripture with you? What do you think they would say or do if you told them life felt too stressful or too heavy for you to deal with alone? How about your mom/dad, brother/sister, or even a friend? Life is a bit easier with people around you, supporting you, providing some peace when you're having trouble finding it yourself. **Write the names of all the people you can call up when you're feeling a bit overwhelmed:**

1. _____

2. _____

3. _____

Now, write out your list on a separate piece of paper. Next to each person, write at least one way you can reach that person—a phone number to text, a profile to message, a landline to call, or even the day of week you always see them and will have a chance to pull them aside to talk. Tape that list to the back of your bedroom door so the next time you feel overwhelmed with life, the next time you want to shut it all out, you can see that list of people and reach out to someone for help finding peace.

MAKE WAVES CHALLENGE

WHISTLE

Time to grade your Swimming Buddy!

DID YOUR GROWN-UP DEVOTIONAL BUDDY MEMORIZE PHILIPPIANS 4:6-7A?

☐ YES   ☐ NO

✗ ....

(sign your name here)

BONUS:

What did you give them for memorizing the verses?

WEEK FOUR

Patience

DAY 1

WHAT IS PATIENCE?

Have you ever been surfing? Well, if you haven't, it's really fun! But I should warn you, it's also pretty hard.

Picture the perfect day: The sun is up. The waves are rolling in. You woke up early and are ready to be the next Kelly Slater (in the 90s, this guy was the Lebron James of surfing)!

Draw a picture of what you would look like hitting the perfect wave:

That's a pretty gnarly[1] (när-lee: *the g is silent*) wave! And whenever we think of surfing, that's what we have in mind. But the truth is, *most* of surfing is just sitting around waiting for the right tide to roll in. Seriously, I've seen guys sitting out there for nearly an *hour* just . . . waiting.

---

1   gnarly = difficult or challenging

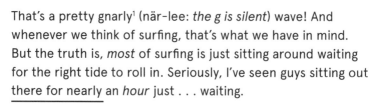

Surfing takes a lot of *patience* (Oh, hey! Another characteristic of the fruit of the Spirit!) It's more about reading how the water is moving and how the wind is blowing than about riding the waves. When you do those things, you'll hit the perfect wave. But if you get upset and start complaining about having to wait or not getting the perfect tide, you'll totally wipeout.

This week, we'll be talking about patience and how God designed us to make waves by showing the world around us the same patience God shows us! We mess up . . . a lot. It has to be frustrating for God to watch us make all our bad decisions. But God is patient with us. God hears our prayers when we're hurting. God never runs away. God is slow to get angry. God's patience with us has made MAJOR waves in the world.

God wants us to do the same. God wants us to be patient with others, with ourselves, and with situations in our lives. God wants us to know the peace that comes with practicing patience. So, let's spend this week practicing being patient!

WHISTLE

MEMORY VERSE CHALLENGE

Everyone should be quick to listen. But they should be slow to speak. They should be slow to get angry.

James 1:19b

DAY 2

HOW DOES GOD SHOW PATIENCE?

Think about your mom or grandpa or teacher when they're super busy. Maybe they're running around packing for a trip, trying to fix a complicated machine, or trying to get a bunch of kids to do just one simple task.

In times like this, have you ever heard a warning like, *"Do not test me right now"*? That's a grown-up giving a hint that they're about to lose their patience. That's when you know they're so exhausted and stressed, they will *not* have the patience for your shenanigans (they may have even used that weird grown-up word "shenanigans" in their warning to you).

Draw a picture of a grown-up in your life losing their patience and the warning they like to give:

Well, since the very beginning, God has been showing us patience.

No really, from the moment Adam and Eve were on this planet, God has been very patient with people.

In Genesis, we read how God created the earth, land, water, sky, animals, and finally humans. Even after all that *work* and incredible expression of creativity, God *still* had patience with Adam and Eve when they chose their own way of doing things.

Adam and Eve were instructed by God not to eat from the tree of the knowledge of good and evil. But you probably know what happened next. They were tempted to eat the fruit from the tree of the knowledge of good and evil . . . and they did. Immediately after eating the fruit, they were filled with shame. But instead of telling God what they did, they hid from God.

> *Then the man and his wife heard the Lord God walking in the garden. It was during the coolest time of the day. They hid from the Lord God among the trees of the garden. But the Lord God called out to the man. "Where are you?" he asked.*
>
> *Genesis 3:8-9*

God was patient with them. God looked for them and had a conversation with them. Yes, Adam and Eve faced consequences for their actions, but God continued loving them.

And that's just one example of God showing patience. *Just think about the number of times you have messed up or made mistakes and God responded with patience.*

The truth is this, God knows everything that's going to happen.

That's why God sent Jesus. God knew we needed a *lot* of patience. So Jesus died and came back to life to reconnect us with our patient, loving God. Jesus continues to wash away our sins or bad decisions over and over again. Talk about being patient with us!

We have the greatest example of patience in Jesus. So, what would it look like to have Jesus-level patience in your life?

I know, I know. You're thinking, "How can I be patient like Jesus? He's perfect and I'm not." I know because I've thought the same thing. And you're right. He is perfect, but Jesus believes in you. He believes that you can follow His example and show the world His love through being patient with others.

I can show patience by:

_____

_____

_____

_____

DAY 3

HOW CAN PATIENCE MAKE WAVES IN MY LIFE?

There are about 6,500 different languages spoken in the world today. But did you know surfers have a language all to themselves? **See if you can match them all to their correct definition on the right page.**

Of all the words you just learned, the number one word that every surfer has to use is one you already know: patience. Patience is the key to getting that awesome wave. If a surfer is too early or impatient for the wave to go in their favor, either they'll not catch the wave or they'll wipeout!

Believe it or not, everyday life is the same. We all have to have the patience to make the right choices—choices that make good waves, not choices that cause us to wipe out. God wants us to show patience when . . .

. . . your mom keeps telling you to make your bed, even though you already know you're supposed to.

. . . your little sister won't stop talking your ear off while you're playing Mario Kart and Bowser is right on your tail.

. . . your teacher has an awesome field trip planned in April, but the school year just started.

MATCHING GAME

Dawny	Lineup	Stoked	Duckdive
Off the hook	Wetties	Wipeout	Pocket

_____ **A.** the act of falling from your board when riding a wave

_____ **B.** the area of the wave that's closest to the curl of the wave

_____ **C.** a technique by which you submerge your board under the water

_____ **D.** the place where surfers sit on their boards and wait for the perfect wave

_____ **E.** surfer speech for a wetsuit

_____ **F.** the feeling of being excited and happy

_____ **G.** going for a surf session very early in the morning

_____ **H.** when the waves are performing extraordinarily well

Dawny (G), Off the hook (H), Lineup (D), Wetties (E), Stoked (F), Wipeout (A), Duckdive (C), Pocket (B)

The key to all of these situations is patience. Patience is believing what you are waiting for is *worth* waiting for. Being patient with your mom is worth it because respecting her is important. Being patient as you wait for an important date is worth it because that moment will be so special.

Not only that, *how* you show patience is key. Being patient all alone can be super tough. But with God, it can be a bit easier. Through the Holy Spirit, God lives inside of you. That means God can help you be patient. God is patient with us, not angry or mad, but rather calm and understanding. With the Holy Spirit's help, we get God's patience too.

What moments in your life have you been patient?

_____

_____

_____

_____

_____

We make waves by showing others our patience for them and by being patient for things in our life. It builds our trust in God as we depend on the Holy Spirit to help us be patient like God is patient with us.

DAY 4

HOW DID PEOPLE IN THE BIBLE SHOW PATIENCE?

What is your favorite season?

- **A.** Spring
- **B.** Summer
- **C.** Fall
- **D.** Winter

Why?

_____

_____

This question can be very tricky because there are so many reasons to love them all! Spring brings beautiful flowers, summer because of vacation and no school, fall the changing of the leaves and PSL (or pumpkin spice lattes for those who don't drink coffee), and winter . . . well, Christmas of course!

Whichever one you chose, we can all agree, waiting for whatever season you enjoy most can feel like a long time . . . especially if you love Christmas and it's March, and you have to endure the heat of the summer and get through Halloween and Thanksgiving just to get to that most wonderful time of the year. Talk about having patience.

I can only assume that when it's not your favorite season, you're just grumpy. Like super grumpy. And the next day, if it hasn't become your favorite time of the year, you continue to be Sir Grumps A Lot. No smiles. No high fives. Just grump.

Wait, wait, wait . . . that's not you? Sweet! That would be a terrible way to live.

But waiting on something good can get kind of tough. This is where patience comes in. Sure, when there's no snow yet or the school year isn't quite over, you can be a bit bummed, but if you're mad about it, you'll miss out on some awesome things like . . .

- → your friends' birthday parties,
- → all the extra dessert you get after dinner,
- → the random family game nights,
- → and all the days off and holidays that happen throughout the year!

But don't worry. You're not alone, there was a man in the Bible who had to wait a LONG time for the one thing that was promised to him and his family . . . a baby.

In Genesis 12, we read that God called a man named Abraham (just like Lincoln) to go to a land called Canaan (Kay-nan). God promised to make a great nation there.

And this great nation would come from his descendants[1]. The only thing was, Abraham and his wife Sarah didn't have any kids, not to mention, Abraham was 75 years old and Sarah was 65 years old!

Here's the wild part . . . when they finally received the gift they were promised, Abraham was 100 years old and Sarah was 90! Talk about patience. They both waited for decades, about twenty-five years, before receiving their first child. After this, the Bible refers to Abraham as a man of faith.

Do you think Abraham and Sarah might have gotten tired while waiting for a baby? Probably. Or frustrated? Maybe. What about angry because it was taking so long? Most likely. But what did they do? They kept their focus on God, and because of that, they were able to help change the world as they knew it.

A person with a bad temper stirs up conflict.
But a person who is patient calms things down.

Proverbs 15:18

This is such a great example of how our faith can build if we continue to focus on God while we're patiently waiting. Reminder: It won't always be easy. It won't always be fun. But it will always be worth it.

---

1   descendants = his kids and kids' kids and kids' kids' kids and . . . you get it.

What are some things in your life that are worth being patient for?

_____

_____

_____

_____

_____

DAY 5

MAKE WAVES

Just for fun, rank the following list of things that challenge your patience: (1 being very hard and 5 being kind of easy)

_____ Getting way too much homework before the weekend

_____ Waiting on your parents to finish up so you can go home

_____ Seeing all your birthday gifts at your party, but not being able to open them yet

_____ Saving money for that new thing you want

_____ Waiting for the last day of school to be over

Some of those are pretty easy to be patient with, but others—like watching the clock in school when there are only five more minutes left before summer break and . . . it . . . takes . . . for . . . ev . . . er . . . for . . . the . . . bell . . . to . . . ring—can be tough. But we're able to lean on God for help to get through those moments. Remember, patience is a quality of the fruit of the Holy Spirit, which means it's from God! And God lives in you through the Holy Spirit! When we ask for God's help, God will help us be patient for moments and with other people.

Over time, waiting will become a bit easier, but you have to practice the wait by not complaining, grumbling, or getting upset when things aren't going your way.

Do everything without complaining or arguing.

Philippians 2:14

MAKE WAVES CHALLENGE

Let's go! I am so over-the-moon excited for you right now! Four weeks down and five more to go! You got this! Now go grab your swimming buddy because it's time to grade them!

DID YOUR GROWN-UP DEVOTIONAL BUDDY MEMORIZE JAMES 1:19B?

☐ YES   ☐ NO

X ....
(sign your name here)

BONUS:

What did you give them for memorizing the verse?

_____

WEEK
FIVE

Kindness

DAY 1

WHAT IS KINDNESS?

List your most valuable items below. You don't need to write the price, just the most valuable things you own. Things you would be *really* upset about losing or breaking. Maybe you have an awesome surfboard, a smartphone, or a really nice pair of socks from your grandma.

1. _____

2. _____

3. _____

4. _____

5. _____

Those are some pretty awesome things!

This week we're talking about a part of the fruit of the Spirit that's all about value. Sure, all of those things you listed are valuable, but kindness is a part of the fruit of the Spirit that's all about seeing the value in *others*—just the way God sees them.

Kindness is showing others they're valuable by how you treat them.

Just like the other characteristics of the fruit of the Spirit, kindness is a gift from God—a gift God wants us to use all the time. Kindness is something that you must choose every single day. And the closer you are to God, the easier it is to choose kindness.

WHISTLE

Let's take a look at what Paul wrote to the people of Colossae:

MEMORY VERSE CHALLENGE

You are God's chosen people. You are holy and dearly loved. So put on tender mercy and kindness as if they were your clothes. Don't be proud. Be gentle and patient.

Colossians 3:12

Paul instructed us to put on kindness like clothes. No, he didn't mean you have to mime getting dressed in kindness like you're playing a game of charades. He simply meant to make kindness part of your daily routine—like putting on clothes. As you're choosing your #OOTD, choose kindness for the day as well.

But what does it look like to choose kindness? Paul told us in the verse above: *Don't be proud. Be gentle and patient.*

So, choosing kindness means choosing not to be proud, to let others shine, to point the spotlight on someone other than yourself. It's giving someone all the space they need to celebrate their wins and feel their losses. Even though you won your baseball tournament over the weekend, it's staying quiet at school on Monday because you found out your friend's pet passed away.

Choosing kindness means choosing to be gentle, choosing gentle words and a gentle attitude, and holding back those harsh, cutting words you sometimes think.

Choosing kindness means choosing to be patient, giving second chances, and not overreacting when others mess up, let you down, or do something differently than you would have.

I know what you're thinking: Those things are easy to say, but they're not always easy to do. It takes work to let go of our pride, to always be gentle with others, and to practice patience.

That's why we have to intentionally choose patience, to put it on each morning like we put on our shoes. **Draw a picture to the right of your #OOTD (outfit of the day). Then write the times you think might be the hardest to show kindness today or this week.** Knowing the possible challenges and choosing kindness anyway comes from the power of God's Spirit!

It's hard not to be proud when . . .

_____

_____

_____

It's hard to be gentle when . . .

_____

_____

_____

It's hard to be patient when . . .

_____

_____

_____

DAY 2

HOW DOES GOD SHOW KINDNESS?

When it comes to surfing, you really don't need a ton of stuff to get going. Outside of learning to swim and getting a ride to the beach, there are only three essential things that each surfer must own: a surfboard, a wetsuit, and surf wax.[1]

So, how much do you think those things cost?

Surfboard:	Wetsuit:	Surf wax:
$ _____	$ _____	$ _____

Check your answers here.

→ Surfboard: $400-$1000

→ Wetsuit: $75-$100

→ Surf wax: $10-$15

That's quite a bit of money! Even though you don't need much to surf, it can still cost a bit to ride the waves. Really, the only thing that's free is the ocean. How cool would it be if you took a trip to the beach and as soon as you sunk your toes in the sand, someone handed you a brand-new surfboard, a

---

1   surf wax = wax that coats your board and protects it in the water.

wetsuit in just your size, a ton of surf wax, and said, "These are yours. Go for it!" That would be righteous, brah!

Have you ever gotten something really valuable for free? If you have, tell the story here. If not, list three things that would be sick to get for free.

1. _____

2. _____

3. _____

Guess what? In the Bible, we can read about how God gave you and me a bunch of stuff for free. (No, God didn't hand out wetsuits.) See if you can find what God gave us for free in the verses below:

The kindness and love of God our Savior appeared. He saved us. It wasn't because of the good things we had done. It was because of his mercy. He saved us by washing away our sins. We were born again. The Holy Spirit gave us new life. God poured out the Spirit on us freely. That's because of what Jesus Christ our Savior has done.

Titus 3:4-6

Did you catch it? Go back and underline Who these verses say God freely gave us.

That's right! God *poured out the Spirit* on us freely! It's like if you walked into your favorite ice cream shop and the owner just started handing out your favorite flavor, but one-hundred-times better! God gives us the Holy Spirit without question. God loves us and wants to be close to us. So if at any point you need kindness or the strength to be kind, all you need to do is ask!

The great thing about kindness is . . . it's always free! Just like all the other parts of the fruit of the Spirit, it costs us nothing to be kind, but it can have a *massive* payoff in the lives of those around us—and in our own lives!

Take a moment to say thank you for all the kind things God has done for you.

But don't stop there! It's also important to thank the people in our lives who are kind to us every day. Maybe that's a parent, sibling, friend, mentor, church leader, or teacher. Go thank the last person who freely poured kindness on you right now!

DAY 3

HOW CAN KINDNESS MAKE WAVES IN MY LIFE?

Just imagine for a minute . . .

Today is the day you've been waiting for. Basketball legend Michael Jordan announced that he has made a brand-new, and final, shoe called the Air Jordan 1 "Make Waves" edition. The shoes are blue and white and signed by Michael Jordan himself. *(For those who don't know who this MJ guy is, let's just say he's the Lebron James of the '90s, and now he makes popular shoes.)*

The shoes look sick in the ads, but the biggest news is, he only made one pair! On top of that, they were shipped to a random shoe store somewhere in the world.

If that really happened, people would go wild! They would search high and low. The news would cover the sneaker search 24/7. Every person, sneakerhead or not, would be looking frantically for them.

Can you imagine how much this shoe would be worth?

- → $1,000?
- → $10,000?
- → $100,000?

→ $1,000,000?

→ Priceless?

Even if the shoe store sold them for $100, which is pretty cheap for Jordan shoes, they would be so valuable—priceless even—simply because there's only one of them. And whoever was lucky enough to find and buy these shoes could resell them for thousands and thousands of dollars. Why?

Because they're one of a kind. They are **rare**!

Now, if that's true about a fake pair of shoes, think about how true it is about *you*. Or your sibling. Or a friend. We're all one of a kind because in the history of the world, God has only made one of you! (Yes, even if you are a twin or triplet.) That makes you rare. That means you are priceless. You are valuable.

God has encouraged us to be kind and compassionate to others. God knows that each of us is one of a kind and just how valuable we are. We need to understand that too, and so did the people who lived back in Bible times. Let's see what Paul wrote to the people of Ephesus:

> *Be kind and compassionate to one another, forgiving each other, just as in Christ God forgave you.*
>
> *Ephesians 4:32 (NIV)*

One of the best things we can do to show others how valuable they are is to follow Jesus' lead. Finding those moments in your day to care for someone, to be kind to someone, or to forgive someone is very important and can make huge waves in the world around you.

What are a few ways you can let those around you know how valuable they are today?

_____

_____

_____

_____

MAKE WAVES

DAY 4

HOW DID PEOPLE IN THE BIBLE SHOW KINDNESS?

Do you have a pet that you rescued from a shelter or the side of the road? Have you ever found a wounded animal and tried to nurse it back to health? Why do you think you (or anyone) does that sort of thing?

Because you see the _____ in every animal.

   A. fleas

   B. value

   C. dinner

Hopefully, you aced that single-question pop quiz. We show kindness to animals—and fellow humans—because we see their value.

When it comes to seeing the value in another person, we have to talk about a royally huge moment from the Bible. This story is found in Exodus 2:1-10 and took place in Egypt during the Old Testament days when the Pharaoh issued a ruling throughout the land.

The pharaoh, or king of Egypt, had made a decree (or law) in the land stating that when Hebrew women gave birth, they were only allowed to let the girls live. They had to throw the baby boys into the Nile River. (Umm . . . not cool, Pharaoh.)

The pharaoh was afraid of the Hebrew boys becoming men and rebelling against him. (The only reason he was afraid of this was because he'd not been kind to Hebrew people for a long time.)

Naturally, Hebrew women weren't so keen on throwing their sons in the river. One Hebrew woman gave birth to a son and hid him from the king for three months. But after three months, she realized she could no longer hide him. He was getting too big, too loud. So, she placed her infant son in a *basket* and sent him down the Nile River. (Nice loophole, Mom.)

At the same time, the daughter of the pharaoh had gone down to the riverbank and seen this baby in the basket. She knew the baby was a Hebrew boy, but she got the baby out of the river and made sure he was taken care of. Later, the Pharaoh's daughter named the boy Moses[1]* and raised him as one of Pharaoh's own sons!

Talk about kindness! The daughter of the king knew that this boy was to be killed, but she saw his worth. She saw his value and not only saved him but made sure he was taken care of as he grew up. That is true kindness. Little did she know, Moses would grow up to be the leader of God's chosen people. He would bring God's people out of slavery and begin their journey into the land God had promised them for generations!

---

1   Moses means to pull out/draw out of water

Has there ever been a moment in your life when someone did something kind out of nowhere, and it meant the world to you? Maybe it even changed the course of your life? Tell about that moment here:

_____

_____

_____

_____

_____

_____

_____

_____

_____

_____

DAY 5

MAKE WAVES

As Christians, we're called to show kindness to everyone we meet. That doesn't mean you have to be best friends with everyone you meet. Inviting the whole world to your birthday party would be a logistical nightmare.

But there are things you can do every day for everyone that would make big waves in the world.

- Smile at everyone you see.
- Notice—and try to help—when someone is having a hard time.
- Stand up for everyone.
- Give compliments and encouragement to everyone.
- Use manners (say thank you and please) with everyone.
- Be a good listener to everyone.

There are also special things you can do throughout your week to make even *bigger* waves of kindness. Over the next few days, you (and anyone else you invite) will be playing Kindness Bingo (on the next page). If you've never played the classic game Bingo, the goal is to check off one whole row of squares vertically, horizontally, or diagonally. Can you guess how you get to check off squares in Kindness Bingo?

You got it: by completing the act of kindness written on the square! So, challenge yourself or your friends and see how quickly you can complete a row of kind acts!

As you play, think about how each act of kindness makes you feel. Think about how it makes the other person feel. Think about how putting more kindness into the world might make waves in the lives of people you've never even met!

MAKE WAVES CHALLENGE

Kindness is one of the best ways to show others how much God loves them, but before you go and change the world with kindness . . .

WHISTLE

Time to grade your Swimming Buddy!

DID YOUR GROWN-UP DEVOTIONAL BUDDY
MEMORIZE COLOSSIANS 3:12?

☐ YES   ☐ NO

✗ ....

(sign your name here)

BONUS:

What did you give them for memorizing the verse?

_____

_____

_____

KINDNESS BINGO

PUT CHANGE IN A VENDING MACHINE	DONATE BOOKS TO A HOSPITAL WAITING ROOM	LET SOMEONE GO AHEAD OF YOU IN LINE
TAKE FLOWERS TO YOUR TEACHER, COACH, OR SMALL GROUP LEADER.	COMPLIMENT AT LEAST FIVE PEOPLE IN ONE DAY	BRING IN YOUR NEIGHBOR'S GARBAGE CANS FOR THEM
MAIL A HANDWRITTEN NOTE TO A FRIEND	LEAVE ONE-DOLLAR BILLS IN THE DOLLAR STORE TOY SECTION	LEAVE A DISH OF FRESH WATER OUT FOR NEIGHBORHOOD DOGS
TAPE BAGS OF POPCORN TO MOVIE RENTAL MACHINES	DONATE TOWELS AND BLANKETS TO AN ANIMAL SHELTER	SMILE AT TEN PEOPLE
DONATE TO A FOOD PANTRY	MAKE SOMEONE ELSE'S BED	PLAY WITH SOMEONE NEW

WEEK

SIX

Goodness

DAY 1

WHAT IS GOODNESS?

Last week we talked about being kind to everyone. This week we're talking about showing God's goodness to others. But what's the difference? Kindness is treating others like they're important—because they are! And goodness is making the decision to do the right thing for others.

What does the Bible say about goodness?

WHISTLE

MEMORY VERSE CHALLENGE

"A good person produces good things from the treasury of a good heart, and an evil person produces evil things from the treasury of an evil heart."

Matthew 12:35 (NLT)

A simpler way of saying it would be . . . a good person will do good things and a person who is not-good, will do not good things. Does that mean a good person can't do bad things? And the other way around? Well, let's discuss. Answer the following questions aloud as you read this. Have you ever . . .

→ made fun of someone? Yes or No?

→ talked back to a grown-up? Yes or No?

→ told someone a lie? Yes or No?

→ taken something that wasn't yours? Yes or No?

→ not apologized even though you knew you were wrong? Yes or No?

Here's the reality. We all make mistakes and sometimes do not-so-good things. Why? Because it's not easy to be good all the time. When we try on our own, we still do the wrong thing sometimes. So, how can we show goodness to others? It's all about that one little phrase in this week's Memory Verse, *"from the treasury of a good heart" (Matthew 12:35 NLT)*.

Treasuries are like little chests or safes. They hold whatever you put in them until you need it. When we put good things in our hearts, it's easier to show goodness to others. **So, what are some good things you can put in your heart? Check off the list below as you find the time to put these good things in your heart's little treasure box:**

_____ Memorize your favorite Bible verses (especially ones that tell you what goodness is!).

_____ Talk to God each day.

_____ Encourage someone (be specific).

_____ Give thanks to God for things in your life.

_____ Ask God for forgiveness for the mistakes you've made.

DAY 2

HOW DOES GOD SHOW GOODNESS?

If you had a restaurant that was popular amongst surfers called "Something Good," what would be on your menu?

Drinks: _____

_____

Snacks: _____

_____

Main Dishes: _____

_____

Desserts: _____

_____

When we go to restaurants for a bite to eat, what we order is all personal preference. You may think pickles are good, but someone else may not. You may think pineapple pizza is good, but others (including me) may not like it at all.

For food, what's "good" may change from one person to the next, but when it comes to God, what's "good" is wonderful to all.

In the Bible, we can read all sorts of examples about how God is good, but one that stands out is the parable (or story) Jesus told about the lost sheep.

Basically, Jesus told the story of a shepherd who had a hundred sheep and lost one. The shepherd left the other ninety-nine sheep to go after the one lost sheep, and when he found the lost sheep, he called all his friends and neighbors to celebrate.

Jesus says it's the same for us. When we're lost and in need of God's goodness, our shepherd (God) will do everything to find us. And when we're found, Heaven celebrates—each and every one of us. Isn't that amazing?

God's goodness is for all. And God showed us the ultimate goodness with Jesus. God sent Jesus for us! In fact, Jesus called Himself the Good Shepherd. Check it out.

> *"I am the good shepherd. The good shepherd gives his life for the sheep."*
>
> *John 10:11*

Not only did Jesus come to Earth to show us God's goodness and how to do good ourselves, Jesus also laid down His own life for us!

Just like Jesus is the Good Shepherd for all of us, God tells you and me to show others the amazing goodness of God too. God wants us to be good to our friends, family, and everyone else we interact with in life.

List three things that you can do to show how good God is:

1. _____

2. _____

3. _____

DAY 3

HOW CAN GOODNESS MAKE WAVES IN MY LIFE?

When was the last time something good happened to you?

How did that make you feel? Choose any emoji that applies to you.

Does that moment inspire you to do good for others?

If it does, that's what I call a ripple effect! A ripple effect is one of the coolest things. If you've ever thrown a rock into a lake or river or have done a cannonball into a pool, you've seen a ripple. It's the echoing waves of water that happen after something or someone has fallen into it.

That same effect happens when we choose to do a good deed for someone. It can inspire someone to be thankful, encouraged, or want to do good too. The best part is, when we show goodness through good deeds to the people around us, we're pointing people to God!

Jesus told us we should be a light in the world. The world will see our good deeds, and it will give God the glory[1].

> *"You are the light of the world. A town built on a hill can't be hidden. Also, people do not light a lamp and put it under a bowl. Instead, they put it on its stand. Then it gives light to everyone in the house. In the same way, let your light shine so others can see it. Then they will see the good things you do. And they will bring glory to your Father who is in heaven."*
>
> *Matthew 5:14–16*

This is such a great reminder of why it's important to do as much good as possible in the world. There will be times people will see the good you're putting into the world and times they won't, but God always sees. And that's all that matters. When you do good, your character grows. Your character gets stronger, and God will continue to use you to make waves of love, to make waves of joy, to make waves of peace, patience, and kindness!

Take a few minutes to talk to God. Tell God you want to shine your light to point others to Jesus.

Thank God for something in your life.

Ask God to forgive you for something wrong you've done.

Ask God to help you do something good for someone else.

---

1   *glory* = high praise

DAY 4

HOW DID PEOPLE IN THE BIBLE SHOW GOODNESS?

Remember week one? It may seem like a year ago (especially if you're like me and you tend to put books down only to pick them back up a year later). Still, think back to week one. Our topic was love. We talked about how the Good Samaritan made waves by demonstrating love. The Good Samaritan is such a *good* story (see what I did there) that it can be an example of love, kindness, and goodness!

But this week, I have *another* story of goodness for you—a story we can find recorded for us in the Bible. It's about a man named Zacchaeus. Yes, Zacchaeus (Za – KEY – Us). That is a wild name! It's almost as wild as the surf terms *cowabunga* or *bodacious*! But, back to the goodness in the story of Zacchaeus.

In Luke 19, Jesus was headed to the city of Jericho when we're introduced to a famous guy named Zacchaeus. Now, when I say famous, I mean *infamous*. People all around town knew who Zacchaeus was and what he did. The reason people knew who Zacchaeus was because he was a tax collector. Tax collectors were people who collected money from others, money those people owed the government. The *enemy* government. In that day, most tax collectors took *more* than was actually owed and put that extra in their own pockets. We don't know if Zacchaeus did that, but it's possible. What we know for sure is that he took money from his people to give to the enemy. So, Zacchaeus was famous . . . for working for the enemy. Yikes. Not the good kind of famous.

Well, Jesus was coming into town, and everyone wanted to see Him, even Zacchaeus. The only problem for Zacchaeus was, he was super short and couldn't see over the crowd. So, he climbed a tree to see Jesus. That's what I call a "make-it-happen attitude." When Jesus saw Zacchaeus sitting in the tree, He told him to come down, and then Jesus went to dinner at Zacchaeus's house.

Jesus' goodness was not well received by the crowd. They started whispering about how Jesus went to eat with a sinner. Remember: Zacchaeus was known because he worked for the enemy. He might have even unfairly taken people's money. But because of Jesus' goodness, Zacchaeus realized his own value and the value in others and decided to do *good*. After dinner with Jesus, Zacchaeus gathered everything he owned and gave half to the poor. He repaid anyone he had stolen from. From then on, Zacchaeus was committed to being and *doing* good.

Jesus' own goodness made pretty big waves.

It's amazing to see someone understand their value because someone else's goodness showed it to them. Have you ever had someone see you the way Jesus saw Zacchaeus? Did they help you through a rough time? Or help you see your bad choices in a different light? Have you had anyone show you goodness like we see from the people we read about in the Bible?

Write that person's name here:

_____

Now if you're able, shoot them a text or call them on the phone to thank them for their goodness!

After you do, draw a shaka sign here:

DAY 5

MAKE WAVES

Remember our Memory Verse Challenge? Have you been memorizing it too? See if you can fill in the words that are missing:

"A _____ person produces _____ things from the treasury of a _____ heart, and an _____ person produces _____things from the treasury of an _____ heart."

Matthew 12:35 (NLT)

You need to fill your treasury with good deeds every day in order to show others goodness. And when we do good deeds, it brings glory to God.

When your friend is having a bad day, try writing them an encouraging note:

"Hey _____ ,

Heard you were having a bad day. I want to let you know, you got this! I hope that tomorrow is a better day! You rock!

From _____ "

Or if someone is having a hard time at school, take a moment to pray for them. Being good to all people all the time is tough, but the more we do these good deeds for others, the easier goodness will come because we're designed to show God's goodness to others!

Close out this week by doing something *good* for someone. Fill in the blanks below to create a game plan! If you can't think of anything, ask a parent for help!

WHO
(Who can I show goodness to?)

_____

_____

WHEN
(When can I show them goodness? Pick a date and time!)

_____

_____

HOW
(How can I show them goodness? You can choose more than one way!)

_____

_____

MAKE WAVES CHALLENGE

Awwwww, yeah! Another week in the books! You know what that means!

WHISTLE

Time to grade your Swimming Buddy!

First things first:

DID YOUR GROWN-UP DEVOTIONAL BUDDY
MEMORIZE MATTHEW 12:35?

☐ YES   ☐ NO

✕ ....

(sign your name here)

BONUS:

What did you give them for memorizing the verse?

....

....

....

MAKE WAVES

WEEK SEVEN

Faithfulness

DAY 1

WHAT IS FAITHFULNESS?

What are your favorite summer Olympic sports? Put a check next to any you love:

☐ Track and Field

☐ Swimming

☐ Gymnastics

☐ Volleyball

☐ Skateboarding

☐ Table Tennis

☐ Basketball

☐ Other: _____

My favorite has to be swimming! Within the past few years, it seems like swimming has been growing in popularity. Just like any other sport, swimmers not only need skill and hard work, but they also need great coaching. And to have great coaching there needs to be a level of trust between the player and coach.

Canadian Olympic bronze medal winner, Kylie Masse, once said this about her training: "Everyone has what works for them. I try to always keep a positive attitude. I trust the process, my coaches, and support systems."

Trust the process. Coaches show up and provide direction and ways for the athletes to improve their skills, even when the athlete can't see the point of the training. Trust is a huge factor in the part of the fruit of the Spirit we're talking about this week: faithfulness. Let's break it down together.

Faith = trusting or believing

Full = completely or containing as much as possible

Ness = state or condition

Faith + Ful + Ness = the state of completely trusting or believing; being completely trustworthy or believable

Great coaches are trustworthy and faithful to their athletes, which makes the athletes trusting and faithful back. In the same way, we should always be able to trust God's faithfulness and be faithful right back.

WHISTLE

MEMORY VERSE CHALLENGE

Faith is being sure of what we hope for. It is being sure of what we do not see.

Hebrews 11:1

We may not be able to see God like we can see everything else in our lives, but we can be sure of God's presence in our lives. God is always faithful. Just like a great coach, we can trust that God has our best interest in mind.

Who has been a faithful coach in your life? It doesn't have to be an actual soccer coach or volleyball coach. A parent, teacher, grandparent, or small group leader can serve as a coach you can trust too! Write the name(s) of your coach(es) below and one way they have "trained" you:

_____

_____

_____

_____

_____

DAY 2

HOW DOES GOD SHOW FAITHFULNESS?

Getting an award for a job well done feels amazing! If you could award yourself with a trophy, medal, or certificate, what amazing thing would it be for? It could be for something you've done or want to do. What would it look like? A trophy or prize? And what "coach" figure in your life would present it to you? **Design it below:**

THIS AWARD IS PRESENTED TO _____
Name

FOR _____
Reason

ON _____ .
Date

COACH: _____
(example: Iron Man or Simone Biles or Mom/Dad)

Just as much as we love being rewarded for doing totally awesome things, we've all probably done some not-so-awesome things.

→ Lying to a parent

→ Sneaking something

→ Saying mean things about someone else

→ Cheating on schoolwork

→ Yelling at a sibling

→ Using words we shouldn't

These wrong things we do are called *sin*.

The awesome thing about God is this: love. God loves us and knows that every day there are opportunities for us to be faithful as well as opportunities for us not to be faithful. But because of God's love and faithfulness to us, no matter what, God stays by our side. Paul wrote this in his letter to the Roman people after Jesus rose from the dead and went to Heaven:

I am absolutely sure that not even death or life can separate us from God's love. Not even angels or demons, the present or the future, or any powers can separate us. Not even the highest places or the lowest, or anything else in all creation can separate us. Nothing at all can ever separate us from God's love. That's because of what Christ Jesus our Lord has done.

Romans 8:38-39

Wow, what an incredible thing! There is *nothing at all [that] can ever separate us from God*. That is one of the best things about God! God wants to be close to us. And because of Jesus, we can be!

God loves you. God loves you. God loves you. There's nothing you can do that will ever change that.

That's how God's faithfulness is shown in our world: God never gives up on us. That's why God sent Jesus to Earth—to show us who God is and to die for our sins so that we can have a relationship with God forever. It's pretty amazing to know we can trust God to always be there for us. God's faithfulness to us deserves a BIG thank you.

Take some time to award God for all the awesome faithfulness:

THIS AWARD IS PRESENTED TO GOD

FOR _____
Reason

ON _____.
Date

DAY 3

HOW CAN FAITHFULNESS MAKE WAVES IN MY LIFE?

When going to the pool, there are always a few rules to follow in order to keep you safe. **Check off any rules you've seen at the pool. Then match the rule to the correct sign or symbol:**

No diving

Don't walk

Poison

Construction ahead

Bumpy road

No smoking

Wet floor

All of those ways to stay safe are great, but we also have to stay safe in our everyday lives. List a few rules you follow to stay safe every day:

_____

_____

_____

Check out this verse from the book of Psalms that talks about another place we can find safety:

God is our place of safety. He gives us strength.
He is always there to help us in times of trouble.
The earth may fall apart.
The mountains may fall into the middle of the sea.
But we will not be afraid.

The waters of the sea may roar and foam.
The mountains may shake when the waters rise.
But we will not be afraid.

Psalm 46:1-3

The first sentence of the passage talks about how God is our safe place. But how can that be when we can't see God like we see everything else in our lives? This is where trust in God's faithfulness to show up and be there for us is important. We don't have to face hard times on our own.

God will always be there to help. God sends people into your life to love and take care of you. All throughout the Bible, you can see and be reminded of God's comfort and love.

God is faithful to you. Always ready to listen. Always with you. Ready to make waves in your life!

God is the best example of how to be faithful. Because of God's faithfulness, we can be faithful to others so they can count on us.

What are a few times you can remember God's faithfulness in your life?

1. When _____,
   (this happened)

   God _____.
   (did this)

2. When _____,
   (this happened)

   God _____.
   (did this)

3. When _____,
   (this happened)

   God _____.
   (did this)

4. When _____,
   (this happened)

   God _____.
   (did this)

DAY 4

HOW DID PEOPLE IN THE BIBLE SHOW FAITHFULNESS?

What's the best thing you could imagine being surprised with? For me, it's a party-sized bag of Cool Ranch Doritos. Wait, no, a free trip to Hawaii. No, no, no, I've got it—a party-sized bag of Cool Ranch Doritos to eat on the plane to my free trip to Hawaii! One can only dream . . .

Anyway, what about you? What would yours be? Rank the following surprises from one to five, with five being the best surprise that could happen:

_____ Birthday party

_____ No school

_____ Trip to the beach

_____ Your favorite meal for dinner

_____ Money from family

_____ Party-sized bag of Cool Ranch Doritos

When Jesus lived on Earth—and even after—there were a ton of surprises that happened to His BFF's, the disciples. But they weren't always the kind of good surprises listed above.

Take, for example, one of Jesus' disciples named Peter. Peter received a huge surprise once by getting thrown into jail for doing absolutely nothing wrong. He was simply faithful to Jesus, and people didn't like that.

After Jesus died on the cross and rose again, some people finally believed He is the Son of God, but others did not. Those people who didn't believe got really upset when the people who believed in Jesus shared about all the great things Jesus did.

Peter was one of the believers telling everyone the incredible things about Jesus. One day, the Roman king of Judea, King Herod, arrested Peter for being faithful to and teaching about Jesus. Herod threw Peter in jail, but Peter was in for a big surprise!

We can read about what happened in the book of Acts:

> *Peter was sleeping between two soldiers. Two chains held him there. Lookouts stood guard at the entrance. Suddenly an angel of the Lord appeared. A light shone in the prison cell. The angel struck Peter on his side. Peter woke up. "Quick!" the angel said. "Get up!" The chains fell off Peter's wrists.*
>
> *Acts 12:6b-7*

So, to recap: Peter was just telling people about Jesus when all of a sudden, he was thrown into jail. Then, he was chillin' in jail, just trying to get some sleep between a couple of guards, probably thinking he was never getting out, when out of the blue, an angel came and woke him up, setting him free from jail! That's wild! Could you imagine what Peter might have felt? Confused. Excited. Relieved.

Draw a picture of how you might have felt if you were Peter:

Peter's faithfulness to God is what got him in jail, but it was God's faithfulness to Peter that got him out. What an example of faithfulness from God and from Peter! Remember, it's especially important to trust in God when things are hard and not going your way.

DAY 5

MAKE WAVES

Coaches help us through all kinds of moments in our lives. They can be . . .

→ church leaders coaching you through your relationship with God,

→ teachers coaching you through school,

→ parents coaching you through life,

→ or coaches coaching you at a sport.

But whatever kind of coach you have in your life, their faithfulness to you and your faithfulness to them is what builds trust. A great way to make huge waves is by appreciating those who are faithful by being faithful to them.

Practicing appreciation has been shown by people in the Bible, including Jesus. When we have amazing people in our lives who champion us and help us become the best, we should let them know how important they are.

Write down three ways you can appreciate your coach, teacher, parent, or church leader and their faithfulness to you: (Some ways can be writing a card, treating them to Starbucks, or making them signs to cheer them on!)

1. _____

2. _____

3. _____

Now, fill out and decorate the postcard on the next page for someone who is faithful to you. Then give it to them as a sign of appreciation next time you see them!

As we grow our relationship with God, we need to put our faith (faith = trusting or believing) in God. Thankfully, God continues to love us, no matter what.

MAKE WAVES CHALLENGE

WHISTLE

Time to grade your Swimming Buddy!

First things first:

DID YOUR GROWN-UP DEVOTIONAL BUDDY MEMORIZE HEBREWS 11:1?

☐ YES　　☐ NO

✕ ....

(sign your name here)

BONUS:

What did you give them for memorizing the verse?

_____

_____

_____

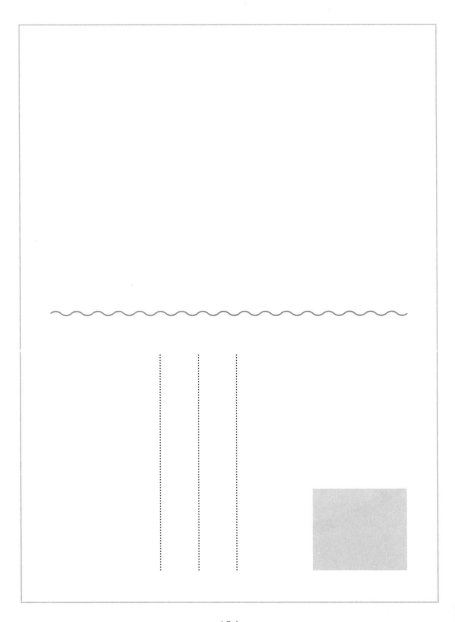

WEEK EIGHT

DAY 1

WHAT IS GENTLENESS?

What's your favorite water activity? It could be a sport, a competition, a hobby. (And yes, frozen water is water too!)

From fishing to hockey, snorkeling to waterparks, water is probably involved in all my most fun days. But you want to know my absolute favorite water game?

The water balloon toss.

That's right. Just tossing a water balloon back and forth with a friend. I think what I love most about it is how exciting and hilarious it can be. It takes the game of catch to the *next level*. It's skill and precision and concentration with the added feeling of anticipation just like cranking a Jack-in-the-Box toy.

The key to water-balloon-toss success is very simple: gentleness. In order to win a classic water balloon toss, you need to have a gentle hand. Toss too forcefully and your whole arm gets soaked. Catch too rigidly and your water balloon is suddenly a puddle at your feet. You have to use your strength to coax the balloon into the air and cushion its fall into your hands.

So why am I talking about water balloons? Because *gentleness* is the second-to-last quality of the fruit of God's Holy Spirit that is mentioned in the book of Galatians.

Just like the water balloon toss, gentleness is key for relationships and how we interact with people around us. We all have our fragile moments. We all need to be handled with care. It takes gentleness to notice when people need some extra care and provide it in a comforting way. Sometimes it isn't easy. Sometimes it feels unnatural, but God can give you the *strength* to be gentle.

Match the gentle responses to the situations below:

Someone sitting alone   listen to them

Someone is sad   offer them a place to sit

Someone drops their ice cream   smile and walk away

Someone behaves unfairly to you   help them clean up

Gentleness is responding to others with care and concern by thinking about what other people need and then putting their needs first. Gentleness is so important in all our relationships. Paul was a guy who came to know Jesus after He had risen from the dead and went to Heaven. Paul spent his life telling people about Jesus. He explained gentleness in this way:

WHISTLE

MEMORY VERSE CHALLENGE

Don't do anything only to get ahead. Don't do it because you are proud. Instead, be humble. Value others more than yourselves. None of you should look out just for your own good. Each of you should also look out for the good of others.

Philippians 2:3-4

My favorite line in these verses is: "Value others more than yourselves." This statement encourages us to care for others because they're valuable. When we value others more than ourselves, we naturally put their needs first. When we value others more than ourselves, we handle them with care—just like a full water balloon.

Think of some times you needed gentleness from others. Maybe after a pet died or you didn't make a team. Maybe after you broke a bone and you literally needed people to be gentle with you.

Now, think of people you know who might need to be handled with a little extra care right now. Spend some time praying for them and try to remember—and remind others—to treat them with gentleness.

DAY 2

HOW DOES GOD SHOW GENTLENESS?

Think back to when you were a kid—well, a little kid. What was your favorite place to play? It could be the park, the playground, or, like me, the beach! Draw it here:

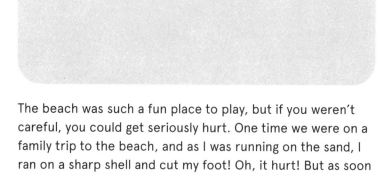

The beach was such a fun place to play, but if you weren't careful, you could get seriously hurt. One time we were on a family trip to the beach, and as I was running on the sand, I ran on a sharp shell and cut my foot! Oh, it hurt! But as soon as my mom heard me in pain, she ran over, cleaned my cut, and placed a Band-Aid on it.

She heard my need and with a gentle heart, cared for me. Have you ever had a time when someone cared for you when you were in need?

What happened? Who cared for you? How did you feel? Write it here:

_____

_____

_____

_____

The awesome thing is this . . . Jesus did the same thing. As you are memorizing the verses for the week with your swimming buddy, check out what Paul wrote about Jesus right after those verses:

As you deal with one another, you should think and act as Jesus did.

In his very nature he was God.

Jesus was equal with God. But Jesus didn't take advantage of that fact.

Instead, he made himself nothing.

He did this by taking on the nature of a servant.

He was made just like human beings.

He appeared as a man.

He was humble and obeyed God completely.

He did this even though it led to his death.

Even worse, he died on a cross!

Philippians 2:5-8

Jesus is God—talk about serious strength. But instead of using His power to force people to listen to Him while He was on Earth, Jesus first listened to those around Him. Jesus took care of others. Jesus didn't even use His strength to get Himself out of dying on the cross!

God saw we needed the ultimate gentleness and sent Jesus to Earth to be with us—to show us God's gentleness in person. The Creator of the entire universe came to Earth to eat, laugh, and cry with the people like you and me.

Jesus chose to be gentle and lay down His life for us. And what Jesus did was the greatest example of God's gentleness. God is so many things—strong, powerful, mighty. But God's greatest show of strength came in the form of gentleness. It came in the Person of Jesus.

There are so many words to describe God. See how many you can find to the right.

WORD SEARCH

strong	good	gentle
peaceful	awesome	patient
loving	holy	kind

```
G P N A I V S U
E A B W S K T A
N T H E C E R L
T I O S G O O D
L E L O V I N G
E N Y M A J G O
R T U E K I N D
P E A C E F U L
```

DAY 3

HOW CAN GENTLENESS MAKE WAVES IN MY LIFE?

This book is called *Make Waves* for a reason. We're called to make waves of change in the world around us. With the Holy Spirit as our guide, we've been challenged to show everyone who God is in our schools, teams, homes, and communities. And when we do that, we make big waves that keep on moving throughout the world.

Now, the thing about waves is that they can be awesome—like in surfing or in a wave pool—and we can create awesome waves by loving others. But waves can also be a bit destructive—like in a hurricane or a tsunami or like that one wave that tumbled you to the bottom of the ocean and you got all scraped up and thought you were going to drown, so you haven't been in the ocean since.

Big, destructive waves usually come from storms that take place out in the ocean. Storms that may start small but get bigger and bigger, taking energy from warmer water until they become a full-on hurricane, making waves that cause a ton of damage and are not enjoyable for anyone.

Just like hurricanes, we can create destructive waves in our lives. Scientists are always trying to figure out how to prevent or stop hurricanes, but lucky for us, we can read some pretty clear instructions in the Bible about how to stop these *life* storms. When we fight our siblings, talk back to our parents, or make choices that hurt someone, we create these life storms. And these life storms can destroy relationships. Here's what the book of Proverbs says:

A gentle answer turns anger away. But mean words stir up anger.

Proverbs 15:1

Words seem so small. It's easy to say, "sorry" when we say something we regret, but words are more powerful than you think. Think about why you use mean words. How are you normally feeling when you choose mean words?

It doesn't matter if you're the one who's angry at someone or if someone is angry at you. Anger hurts. No matter who you are. That's why choosing gentle words that put the other person first is so important.

So, the million-dollar question is: Where do gentle words come from when you don't feel like being gentle? You aren't the only person to ask that question. I've even asked it. But the simple answer is this: from God.

We've been talking about the Holy Spirit and how God sent the Holy Spirit to help and guide us. When we can't think of the words to say, asking the Holy Spirit to help is the best answer. The Holy Spirit can remind you of Bible stories and verses to help you speak gentler. The Spirit can help calm an angry attitude and remind you of what's most important: the relationship, the other person, their value.

God wants to help you become gentler, to get rid of your anger, and to help others around you get rid of theirs too.

Let's practice asking the Holy Spirit to guide our choices, to help us speak gentler, and to be less angry. Take a few minutes to write out a prayer you can be reminded of next time you feel those mean words begging to come out.

Dear Holy Spirit,

_____

_____

_____

_____

_____

Thank You,

DAY 4

HOW DID PEOPLE IN THE BIBLE SHOW GENTLENESS?

One of the best things about growing up is all the new opportunities that come with age. Riding a bike without training wheels, getting your own phone, being able to swim in the deep end of the pool. I don't know about you, but when I was a kid, one of my summer highlights was going to the pool and passing the swimming test to swim in the deep end.

What are your favorite swimming pool activities? Rank the following: (1 being great and 4 being okay)

_____ Cannonball contest

_____ Diving board

_____ Chicken fight

_____ Water slide

Have you ever gone to the pool so stoked to dive into your favorite pool activity when your parents suddenly ask you to watch your younger brother, sister, or cousins? It can be a bit of a disappointment, but the truth is, your little sibling or cousin probably loves the idea of getting to play with you.

There is Someone we can read about in the Bible who was not at all embarrassed to be around little kids: Jesus. Check out this time that Mark wrote about:

People were bringing little children to Jesus. They wanted him to place his hands on them to bless them. But the disciples told them to stop. When Jesus saw this, he was angry. He said to his disciples, "Let the little children come to me. Don't keep them away. God's kingdom belongs to people like them. What I'm about to tell you is true. Anyone who will not receive God's kingdom like a little child will never enter it." Then he took the children in his arms. He placed his hands on them to bless them.

Mark 10:13-16

Jesus wasn't too cool or too busy to hang out and appreciate those younger than Him. Was Jesus cool? Yeah. Did Jesus probably have important things to do? Yeah again. But as we read in these verses, Jesus showed us how important it is to care for those who are younger than you. He gave us a great example of gentleness: stopping to pay attention to those who may not have the loudest voices. Jesus chose to spend time with someone younger because they matter.

This isn't the only place in the Bible that shows the value of those who are younger. Paul also told his young friend Timothy not to let anyone look down on him because he was young (1 Timothy 4:12). And I say the same to you. You don't have to wait to be an adult to care for kids or those younger than you. There are so many people in this world who need a strong person to show them gentleness and care.

Jesus saw an opportunity to spend time with younger people, to be gentle and caring. So, let's be like Jesus!

Spend time with a younger sibling, cousin, neighbor, or friend. Check off these things once you do them:

_____ Allow them to share a thought or story and really listen to them.

_____ Read a book or play a game with them.

_____ Ask if there is something you can help them with.

MAKE WAVES

DAY 5

MAKE WAVES

Gentleness is a such a fascinating thing. With water balloons, we need to be gentle with our touch to protect the balloon. But when it comes to people, we need to be gentle with more than just our actions.

Everything you do, everything you say (including your thoughts) can be gentle or rough. Ultimately, gentleness is a way of being. When you're gentle, everything about you shows others that they're safe and cared for when they're around you. When you're a gentle person, others know they matter. In the book of Titus, Paul shared with us how we should act:

> *Tell them not to speak evil things against anyone. Remind them to live in peace. They must consider the needs of others. They must always be gentle toward everyone.*
>
> *Titus 3:2*

We must always be gentle to everyone. We're able to make others feel safe and cared for in so many ways. We consider the needs of others with our thoughts, our words, our expressions, and our actions. Even when we don't feel like it, we must be gentle to everyone. Always. That's a pretty high bar, a lofty goal. Just remember, the best way to be gentle in the times when you don't want to is to spend time with God. The more time you spend talking to God, reading the Bible, learning about Jesus, and listening to the Holy Spirit, the more gentleness will come out of you.

What are some ways you can show gentleness with . . .

your words: _____

_____

your actions: _____

_____

your facial expressions: _____

_____

your thoughts: _____

_____

One of the best ways to make waves is by responding to others with care and concern by thinking about what other people need and then putting their needs first. That is gentleness!

MAKE WAVES CHALLENGE

WHISTLE

Time to grade your Swimming Buddy!

First things first:

DID YOUR GROWN-UP DEVOTIONAL BUDDY
MEMORIZE PHILIPPIANS 2:3-4?

☐ **YES** ☐ **NO**

X ....

(sign your name here)

BONUS:

What did you give them for memorizing the verses?

_____

_____

_____

MAKE WAVES

WEEK NINE

Self-Control

DAY 1

WHAT IS SELF-CONTROL?

Let's do a quick recap of the parts of the fruit of the Spirit we've talked about so far (no peeking at the past chapters):

1. _____

2. _____

3. _____

4. _____

5. _____

6. _____

7. _____

8. _____

9. _____

So, what's the ninth characteristic of the fruit of the Holy Spirit? Self-control. Why is self-control so important?

When we think about the other characteristics of the Holy Spirit's fruit, we can understand why we need them. Like love—it's important because God loves all people. We need patience because God is patient with us every day. But why do we need self-control?

What do you think self-control is? As a part of the fruit of the Spirit, why do you think it's so important?

_____

_____

_____

_____

_____

In surfing, there are times when you know you need to come back to shore because the waves are too dangerous, or the sun is setting, and you won't be able to see.

In your daily life, self-control can be choosing healthy food instead of choosing junk food. (This one is tough for me too. I love cool ranch Doritos and could eat a whole bag all by myself, but is that what's best for me? Not so much.) Self-control can also be about what you watch on television or what you spend your money on. All of those examples are things you can control. But what about when things are outside your control? How do you react when things aren't going your way and you're disappointed?

Self-control is basically choosing to do what you should do even when you don't want to do it.

It can be really tough, but this week we're going to see how Jesus showed self-control. We're going to learn how to lean on the Holy Spirit when self-control gets hard. But first, check out what Paul wrote to the people of Philippi (where the Philippians lived):

WHISTLE

MEMORY VERSE CHALLENGE

Finally, my brothers and sisters, always think about what is true. Think about what is noble, right and pure. Think about what is lovely and worthy of respect. If anything is excellent or worthy of praise, think about those kinds of things.

Philippians 4:8

There are a lot of things out in the world and in our lives that are outside of our control. What teachers you have at school or where your home is located. If your parents are together or if they're separated. There are so many things that can be difficult in our lives, no matter how self-controlled you are. That's why Paul gave a few pieces of help.

He started by encouraging us to control our thoughts and the things that enter our minds. If you think about something long enough, it might begin to change the way that you act towards yourself or others or even God. So, Paul coached us to think about good and pure things.

Put a star next to thoughts that would pass Paul's test:

_____ "We may have lost, but at least my team played well."

_____ "Nobody cares about that girl at school."

_____ "I'm way smarter than my brother."

_____ "I'm so grateful that my dad cooks dinner."

_____ "I have the worst teachers."

_____ "I'll never be able to do great things; I stink."

_____ "My friends are the kindest people."

DAY 2

HOW DOES GOD SHOW SELF-CONTROL?

Have you ever been *hangry*?

Hangry (adj.): cranky and irritable because of hunger.

Hungry + Angry = Hangry

I don't know about you, but when I'm hangry, it's really hard to have self-control. It's hard to control my words. It's hard to control my attitude. It's hard to control how many cool ranch Doritos I eat. But no matter how out-of-control we feel, we have the Holy Spirit with us to give us the strength to show self-control.

The Holy Spirit is God's very Spirit! The Holy Spirit can help us live like Jesus did, with self-control! One of the reasons Jesus came to Earth was to show us how to live. He faced hard things just like we do and had to make choices just like we do.

One particular time in Jesus' life, He had every reason to be hangry and lose control. But if you know anything about Jesus, you probably know the answer to this question:

Did Jesus (circle your answer) . . .

let His hanger win?   **or**   show self-control?

Let's find out!

A few things to remember before reading this story:

→ Jesus is completely and fully God.

→ Jesus never sinned.

→ At this point, Jesus was fasting, so that meant He hadn't eaten any food for many days, which can make a person hungry, tired, and cranky.

This story comes from the book of Matthew, the first book in the New Testament, chapter four, verses one through eleven. I encourage you to read the whole story, but I'll summarize it for you.

After Jesus was baptized, He was led by the Holy Spirit to fast in the desert. (Fasting is when you don't eat in order to focus on God by praying and trusting that God will give you all you need. It's a way to connect closer with God.) As Jesus was fasting for 40 days and nights, the devil came to tempt Him.

The devil tempted Jesus three times: one time to make food so He could have something to eat; a second time to jump off a cliff to see if God would save Him; and a third time to have Jesus bow down to him and receive land and authority. Even though Jesus was really hangry, Jesus refused all three and said, "No!"

Now, the things that Jesus was tempted with are a bit different than what we're tempted with. But they were significant temptations for Jesus. It's comforting to know that when we face temptations, Jesus knows what it's like to be tempted too. He knows that it can be hard to make the right choices. He also understands how awesome it feels to make the right choice. Since His Spirit lives in us, He can help us make the right choices and show self-control, even when it's hard. In fact, He loves to help because He loves you so much!

Take a minute to complete the maze to the right, avoiding the "temptations" blocking your path. As you find your way, think about how good it would feel to make your way through a whole day with self-control.

DAY 3

HOW CAN SELF-CONTROL MAKE WAVES IN MY LIFE?

If you could own a boat, what would it look like? Draw it below, and describe all of its top-of-the-line features.

_____

_____

No matter how state-of-the-art or up-to-date your boat is, there are a couple of really important parts every boat—from a tiny fishing boat to a luxury cruise ship—must have. One of them is a _rudder_. The rudder is the part at the back of the boat that helps control the direction of the boat.

This piece is small in comparison to the rest of the boat, but it's so powerful. It can change the direction of a huge ship. That is why James used it as an example when talking about the power of our words.

> *Indeed, we all make many mistakes. For if we could control our tongues, we would be perfect and could also control ourselves in every other way.*
>
> *We can make a large horse go wherever we want by means of a small bit in its mouth. And a small rudder makes a huge ship turn wherever the pilot chooses to go, even though the winds are strong.*
>
> *James 3:2-4 (NLT, emphasis added)*

The words we choose to say will determine the direction of our life. Our words are one of the best areas in which to practice self-control. Because it's so easy to lose control with our words, it's important to remember how powerful they are.

When things weren't going your way, have you ever:

- → lied to your parent?
- → said mean words to a friend?
- → talked poorly to a sibling?

Our words have the power to make friendships or to break them. Our words have the power to keep us out of trouble or to get us into it. In sports, our words have the power to build team spirit or to break it down. And our words have the power to lift people up (including yourself) by encouraging them or to tear people down by insulting them.

If we can control the tongue—what we say—we're capable of controlling ourselves in all other ways.

I understand that controlling our words might be easier for some people than it is for others, but that's where God comes in. God's power can help you have self-control. That's why God gave us the Holy Spirit—to teach and guide you and me. So, when you need help with your words, with self-control, with anything, you can ask God's Spirit inside of you for help!

Write a prayer asking God to help you control your words or to help you have self-control when you need it most:

DAY 4

HOW DID PEOPLE IN THE BIBLE SHOW SELF-CONTROL?

Wow! Look at us! We've nearly made it to the end of this book. How do you feel? Do you feel like a surfing expert yet? Do you feel like a fruit-of-the-Spirit expert? (One of those is probably more important than the other.) Still, let's cover one last key to surfing (and any sport for that matter): reflexes.

A reflex is something you do automatically without thinking. There are natural reflexes like jumping and screaming when you get scared or laughing when you hear something funny. And there are learned reflexes like the reflexes good surfers have: riding waves, standing on the board when it's time, balancing on the board. Sometimes our reflexes are good, like when we grab a younger sibling before they step into the street without looking. But sometimes our reflexes get us in trouble, like when we are so frustrated with the video game we're playing we throw the remote across the room.

Let's look at a time in the Bible when one of Jesus' friends had a reflex to protect Jesus—but maybe it was a reflex that needed a little self-control. Jesus was in the garden talking with His friends right before He was killed. Matthew, one of Jesus's BFFs, wrote about this in his book. Check it out.

*While Jesus was still speaking, Judas arrived. He was
one of the 12 disciples. A large crowd was with him.
They were carrying swords and clubs. The chief priests
and the elders of the people had sent them. Judas,
who was going to hand Jesus over, had arranged a
signal with them. "The one I kiss is the man," he said.
"Arrest him." So Judas went to Jesus at once. He said,
"Greetings, Rabbi!" And he kissed him. Jesus replied,
"Friend, do what you came to do."*

*Then the men stepped forward. They grabbed Jesus
and arrested him. At that moment, one of Jesus'
companions reached for his sword. He pulled it out
and struck the slave of the high priest with it. He cut off
the slave's ear.*

*"Put your sword back in its place," Jesus said to him.
"All who use the sword will die by the sword. Do you
think I can't ask my Father for help? He would send an
army of more than 70,000 angels right away. But then
how would the Scriptures come true? They say it must
happen in this way."*

Matthew 26:47-54

Wow, talk about a reflex! First, Peter jumped to protect
Jesus by cutting off the servant's ear (yikes). Then, Jesus
automatically showed self-control and rode it out. (Jesus
healed the servant's ear, by the way.) Jesus could have
easily asked God to send all the angels to come and help,
but He didn't.

Jesus understood the importance of showing self-control. And because of His self-control in this instance and again as He was placed on the cross, we're able to have a relationship with God that lasts forever. Jesus' self-control is key to anyone's relationship with God.

In those moments when your reflexes are to do the opposite of self-control, remember that the Holy Spirit is there to help you, to help you focus on your actions and responses. Take some time to answer the following questions, **"How could the Holy Spirit help you respond when . . ."**

. . . your best friend tells a lie about you?

_____

. . . you were blamed for something you didn't do?

_____

. . . your homework isn't done, but it's time to turn it in?

_____

. . . your video games are taken away?

_____

. . . your team loses the championship game?

_____

DAY 5

MAKE WAVES

You did it. You did IT! Welcome to the last day of the last week. I knew you could do it!

Find a nice, comfortable place to read. I'll wait. No, seriously, this will be awesome if you find a place that's a feel-good space.

Okay. You ready?

Take a moment to think about all you've accomplished up to this point. Maybe you've made a plan to show self-control or to have patience or to love others better. Maybe you made a goal to complete a devotional and you're almost there!

All athletes including surfers, swimmers, or runners have goals that they're working hard to achieve.

What goals do you think Olympic swimmers have?

To help them reach their goals, Olympic athletes have trainers. They definitely practice every day. They're committed, and they have self-control. Here's what Paul wrote about self-control:

All athletes are disciplined in their training. They do it to win a prize that will fade away, but we do it for an eternal prize. So I run with purpose in every step. I am not just shadowboxing. I discipline my body like an athlete, training it to do what it should. Otherwise, I fear that after preaching to others I myself might be disqualified.

1 Corinthians 9:25–27 (NLT)

Training and discipline can lead athletes to winning championships, but imagine what would happen if we trained and were as disciplined in our relationship with God as Olympic swimmers are with their sport? What would happen if we changed our daily routines to reach the goal of growing closer to Jesus and using self-control to achieve those goals?

Take some time to write out how you can practice each of these parts of the fruit of the Spirit each day:

Love _____

Joy _____

Peace _____

Patience _____

Kindness _____

Goodness _____

Faithfulness _____

Gentleness _____

Self-Control _____

As the journey comes to a close, it's so important to remember you're not on this journey alone. You have the single greatest coach ever—God! And God gave you the Holy Spirit to live inside of you and help you. As you pray, read the Bible, learn more about God, and put all this into practice with God, others, and yourself, you'll begin to see that all your hard work is worth it!

My final challenge for you is one that will take some time to finish, but it can potentially stay with you for the rest of your life!

Since we've been talking about coaching, training, choices, discipline, and making waves, I'd like you to write out a good habit that you'd like to get into. It can be anything from making your bed in the morning to cutting back on watching YouTube to reading a Bible verse or praying before you sleep each night.

If you're stumped for an idea, go and ask a friend or an adult for one and write it below:

I want to _____

It has been said that it takes about a month to develop a habit, good or bad, so the more you do something, the more it becomes a reflex. After thirty days, you'll stop thinking about it and just do it. So go ahead and just do it! Use the chart below to help you keep track of your progress. Start on a Sunday, and after completing your goal every day, fill in the box.

Remember, you got this. As your greatest book cheerleader, I believe in you! But more importantly—God believes in you! When you put these parts of the fruit of the Spirit into practice, you can indeed make waves in the world around you!

WHISTLE

MAKE WAVES CHALLENGE

Buddy System! Don't forget your very last chance to grade your Swimming Buddy!

DID YOUR GROWN-UP DEVOTIONAL BUDDY
MEMORIZE PHILIPPIANS 4:8-9?

☐ YES ☐ NO

✗ ....

(sign your name here)

BONUS:

What did you give them for memorizing the verse?

_____

_____

_____

HABIT TRACKER

The habit I am keeping track of is:

In the space below, place a star or shaka for each
day you successfully complete your habit.
Thirty days may seem a lot, but you can do it!

DAY 1	DAY 2	DAY 3	DAY 4	DAY 5	DAY 6
DAY 7	DAY 8	DAY 9	DAY 10	DAY 11	DAY 12
DAY 13	DAY 14	DAY 15	DAY 16	DAY 17	DAY 18
DAY 19	DAY 20	DAY 21	DAY 22	DAY 23	DAY 24
DAY 25	DAY 26	DAY 27	DAY 28	DAY 29	DAY 30

Help your kid build an everyday faith and make the most of the time you already spend together.

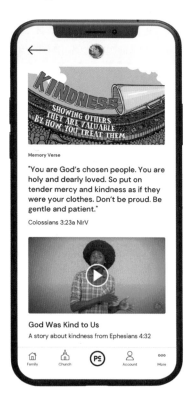

Download the Parent Cue app for free
in the App Store or Google Play Store.

ParentCue.org/app